THE WORLD OF
Animals

THE WORLD OF
Animals

WORLD INTERNATIONAL PUBLISHING LIMITED
MANCHESTER

Contents

Above: Charles Darwin was born in 1809, the son of a Shrewsbury doctor. Having abandoned careers in medicine and the church, he joined HMS *Beagle* as ship's naturalist. His voyages took him all round the world and helped inspire his theories of evolution.

Galapagos Islands

Evolution in Action

Nowadays, evolution is an accepted fact, but it has not always been so. Once, people thought that life arose spontaneously from things like mud, water and air. The Biblical idea of creation was also widely accepted until scientists like Charles Darwin began to introduce new ideas.

Darwin's studies led him to believe that the present-day variety of life on earth had developed from much simpler creatures which lived long ago but had gradually died out, being replaced by more complex ones which were better suited to their environment. Only the most successful animals and plants survived and passed their characters on to their offspring. His ideas were criticized and ridiculed at the time, especially by the church, but he is now known to have been correct about many of his ideas concerning evolution.

Above: During his visit to the Galapagos, Darwin observed remarkable variation in the finches. On the widely separated islands there were separate races. Darwin suggested that all the races had evolved from the same original stock, a species from South America, and that each had adapted to the particular conditions on each island.

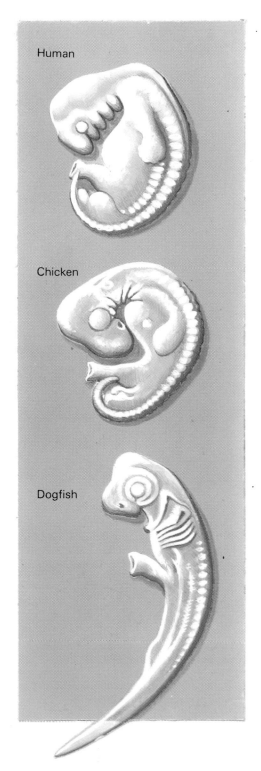

Below: Although no-one would confuse the adult forms of man, chicken and dogfish, it would take an expert to identify their embryos. Darwin suggested that the reason for their similarities was that they are all descended from a common ancestor and, during their development, they go through all the stages of evolution. All vertebrate embryos share many similar features as they develop, looking very much alike at some stages. At an early stage all embryos have gill pouches on their heads, a feature only retained in the adult form by fishes.

Human

Chicken

Dogfish

Studying Evolution

Of the countless millions of animals and plants which have lived and died on this earth before us, a small number died in places where their remains could be preserved as fossils until the present day. Some animals and plants lend themselves to fossilization because of their tough bodies. This is why there is an abundance of fossil pollen, and numerous species of shellfish. By examining changes in the fossil species and relating these to the geological time scale, we can begin to piece together the story of evolution – a process which still goes on today.

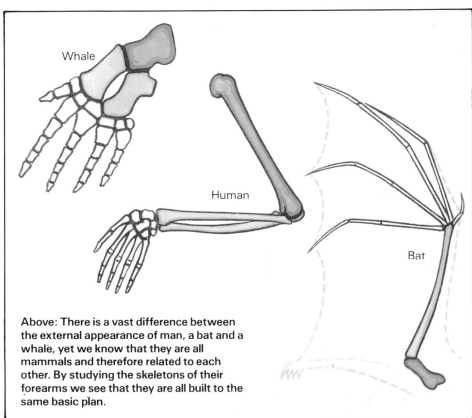

Whale

Human

Bat

Above: There is a vast difference between the external appearance of man, a bat and a whale, yet we know that they are all mammals and therefore related to each other. By studying the skeletons of their forearms we see that they are all built to the same basic plan.

After travelling widely throughout the world and making detailed observations abroad and at home on domesticated animals, Darwin proposed that all life on earth had evolved gradually from the simplest forms over a vast period of geological time. As evidence for his theories he used fossil records, the 'artificial selection' of breeders of domestic pigeons, and his observations on adaptations of species on isolated islands.

In his book 'The Origin of Species', published in 1859, he explained his ideas about natural selection. Animals and plants produce a vast number of offspring in each generation, far more than are needed to maintain a stable population of the species. Most of the young die before they reach adulthood. Darwin proposed that only those most able to survive would do so, the rest would be 'selected out' by nature.

Animals of Long Ago

The first animals appeared on earth many millions of years ago. Their remains sometimes become preserved in rocks. When this happens the remains are known as fossils. By studying fossils, scientists have discovered almost everything they know about the animal life of long ago.

Life began in the oceans. The first forms of life were small, primitive creatures rather like the sponges and jellyfishes of today. In time, larger creatures such as crabs evolved. Then fishes appeared in the seas. Some of these fishes were huge, armour-plated monsters which preyed on other sea creatures.

Eventually fishes evolved which could breathe air. From them developed animals which were able to live both on land or in the water. These were the amphibians, the ancestors of the salamanders, frogs and toads. They first appeared about 350 million years ago.

Once the land had been conquered by animals, other creatures evolved. Next to arrive were the reptiles. For many millions of years, conditions on earth were exactly right for the reptiles, and they flourished in many parts of the world.

Right: *Pteranodon* was a huge flying reptile that lived during the Cretaceous Period, some 130 million years ago. It had a wingspan of about 7 metres. *Pteranodon* probably clambered up on to cliffs and launched itself into the air to soar and glide over the sea. *Pteranodon* had a long bony crest at the back of its head to help counter-balance the huge beak.

Far right: *Alamosaurus* lived in parts of Europe and North America during the Cretaceous Period. It was a large plant-eating dinosaur. *Tyrannosaurus* (the name means 'tyrant lizard') is shown here attacking *Alamosaurus*. *Tyrannosaurus* was the biggest carnivorous reptile ever to have lived. It stood over 6 metres tall.

Left: About one and a half million years ago, great ice sheets from the North Pole crept over many parts of the northern hemisphere. To keep warm, animals such as the woolly mammoth shown here grew long coats. Other shaggy coated animals included the woolly rhinoceros and the cave bear. The sabre-toothed tiger was one of several meat-eating animals which preyed on creatures at this time.

Pteranodon   Alamosaurus   Tyrannosaurus

The biggest reptiles were the dinosaurs. Dinosaurs ruled the earth for about 130 million years. Giant plant-eating reptiles wallowed in the swamplands, browsing on vegetation. On dry land herds of horned dinosaurs roamed about. Many of these plant-eating dinosaurs fell prey to ferocious carnivores like *Tyrannosaurus.*

Some reptiles took to the air, gliding about on leathery wings. Others returned to the sea to feed on fishes and other marine creatures. About 65 million years ago, however, most of the reptiles suddenly died out.

The Age of Mammals

By the time most of the reptiles had died out, the mammals and birds had already evolved. The mammals quickly filled all the habitats occupied by the reptiles. The first mammals were small, mouse-like animals. In time many other kinds of mammal also appeared. Some of these were plant-eaters and others became carnivorous, feeding on the plant-eaters. Today, the mammals are the dominant animals on earth.

Scientists have found fossil bones from many of these early mammals. We know that some were gigantic. There were ground sloths bigger than elephants, and a giant rhinoceros called *Baluchitherium* that was nearly as tall as a house.

Below: Some animals have become extinct in more recent times. The dodo, a bird about the size of a turkey, was once found on Mauritius island in the Indian Ocean. When sailors from visiting ships landed on the island they stole its eggs and killed the birds for food. The last dodo was killed little more than 200 years ago.

9

Seal

Musk ox

Polar bear

World Wildlife

Skunk

NORTH AMERICA

Bald eagle

Puma

About 200 million years ago, when dinosaurs roamed the Earth, the continents were joined together in a vast supercontinent called Pangaea. But slowly the continents drifted apart and animals living on one land mass became separated from those living on another. Each group of animals continued to change – to *evolve* – but, isolated from each other, they evolved in different ways. This is why, today, certain animals are found only on certain continents; why, for example, kangaroos are found only in Australia and llamas only in South America. The map shows animals typical of each area.

Fox

EUROPE

Badger

Swallow

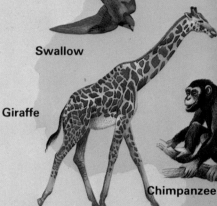

Giraffe

Chimpanzee

Anaconda

SOUTH AMERICA

Scarlet macaw

Sloth

Llama

Armadillo

NORTH AMERICA

Only a narrow stretch of water separates North America from Asia. Often in the past the two land masses have been joined by a land bridge, and animals have been able to pass from one to the other. For this reason, many of the animals found in North America are closely related to those found in Asia and Europe.

Springbok

SOUTH AMERICA

South America has many animals found nowhere else in the world. Some are quite strange in both appearance and behaviour, such as the sloth, spending its days hanging upside-down in the trees, or the toothless anteater, rummaging through ant hills with its long nose. There is also a wealth of beautiful birds such as the scarlet macaw in the tropical rain forests.

Elk

Crane

Wild boar

Wolf

Giant panda

ASIA

Indian elephant

Camel

AFRICA

EUROPE AND ASIA

Many people live in Europe and Asia, and much of the land is farmed, so the larger wild animals are mostly confined to nature parks. But some animals, such as the fox, have adapted to living among people. Others, such as the giant panda, live only in the deepest parts of the forest.

Tiger

Zebra

Bird of paradise

AFRICA

The grasslands of Africa have the most varied collection of large grazing animals in the world – including the giraffe, elephant, rhinoceros, antelopes and many others. These animals and the carnivores which prey on them roam free in vast national parks.

Lion

Kangaroo

Koala

Rhinoceros

AUSTRALASIA

Australia was the first continent to break away from Pangaea. It did so at a time when most of the world's mammals reared their young in pouches. These animals, called marsupials, flourished in Australia, but soon became extinct in other parts of the world. The koala and kangaroo are both marsupials, and are found only in Australia. The tuatara, a reptile found in New Zealand, is the nearest living relative of the great dinosaurs.

Emu

Tuatara

AUSTRALIA

Kiwi

NEW ZEALAND

Animal Lives

There are well over one million different kinds of animals, and they live on almost every part of the Earth's surface. There is animal life in caves, in deserts, and in the deep oceans. Only the frozen wastes of Antarctica and the highest and bleakest mountains are without animals – and even then, a few insects and spiders manage to exist on the coast of Antarctica, while swifts have been seen flying not far from the top of the world's highest mountain, Everest.

Naming Animals

Animals are often grouped together according to their similarities. This is known as classification. For example, some animals live in water, some on land; some are meat-eaters, some eat plants, and some eat both. Zoologists, the people who study animals, classify them according to the structure of their bodies. The simplest scientific group is the *species*, animals that are basically alike and breed among themselves. Similar species are grouped in *genera* (singular *genus*), genera are grouped in *families*, families in *orders*, orders in *classes*, and classes in *phyla* (singular *phylum*). All the phyla together make up the animal kingdom. Every group, from species to phylum, has a Latin name. In this way zoologists can give a name to every different kind, even those which share the same common name: for example, there are 4,000 species called hoverflies!

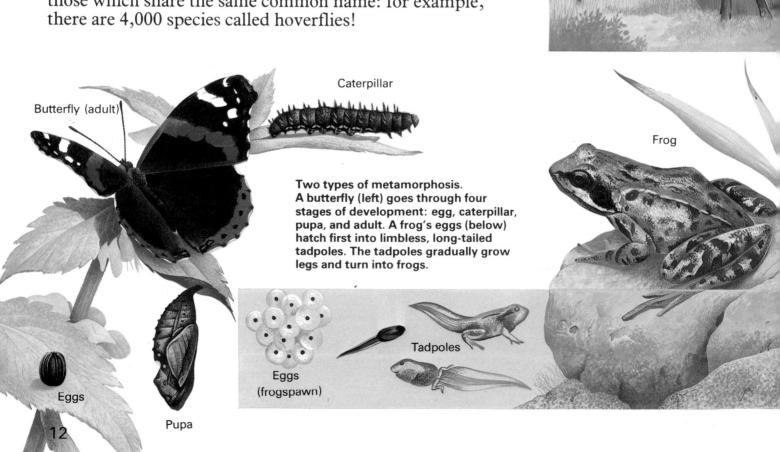

Butterfly (adult)

Caterpillar

Frog

**Two types of metamorphosis.
A butterfly (left) goes through four stages of development: egg, caterpillar, pupa, and adult. A frog's eggs (below) hatch first into limbless, long-tailed tadpoles. The tadpoles gradually grow legs and turn into frogs.**

Eggs

Pupa

Eggs (frogspawn)

Tadpoles

Top left: The cuckoo lays its egg in another bird's nest. The foster bird rears the cuckoo chick, which pushes the other chicks out of the nest.

Top centre: Some species of fish look after their eggs by carrying them around in their mouths until they hatch – and the very young fish also shelter in their mother's mouth.

Top right: When the weather is cold and food is scarce, animals such as the dormouse go into a deep, trance-like sleep, known as *hibernation*.

Left: Deer live in herds. They are usually peaceful animals, but during the rutting (mating) season the males fight each other for possession of the females, clashing their antlers together in fierce combat.

CHANGING SHAPE

Some animals go through a series of changes in shape before they become adults. This process is known as *metamorphosis*, from two Greek words meaning 'change of body'.

Butterflies and many other kinds of insects undergo a four-stage process. The insect starts life as an egg, and hatches into a larva (the larva of a butterfly is called a caterpillar). It spends a large part of its life as a larva, then shuts itself up in a case called a pupa, which it makes of silk. In the pupal stage the insect's body changes tremendously. Eventually it emerges as an adult.

Some insects, such as dragonflies, go through three stages: egg, nymph and adult. The nymph is similar to the adult and grows in size without changing shape.

Animals and Their Young

Wild animals have just two objectives in life: getting enough to eat, and finding a mate and breeding. Most animals move about for these purposes, though a few, such as corals, spend most of their lives fixed in one spot, filtering their food from the water in which they live.

All animals reproduce themselves. Some of the very simplest creatures, called protozoa, just divide to make two 'daughter cells'. Sponges throw out buds, which break off to form new individuals. But most animals reproduce sexually, by the mating of a male and a female. A female produces cells called eggs, and a male produces cells called sperm. When one of each kind of cell comes together they unite, and a new individual grows.

Many animals, including most fish and insects, never see their young. They lay and fertilize their eggs, and then leave them. Other animals look after their young until they are old enough to fend for themselves.

The World of Insects

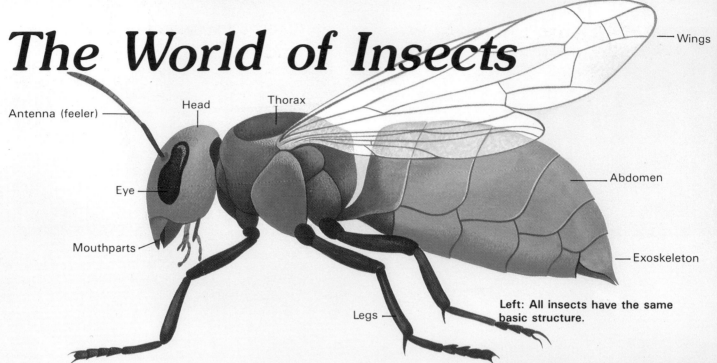

Antenna (feeler)
Head
Thorax
Wings
Eye
Abdomen
Mouthparts
Exoskeleton
Legs

Left: All insects have the same basic structure.

Insects are the most numerous and widespread group of animals on earth. There are more species of insect than all the rest of the species in the Animal Kingdom put together. Over a million different kinds have been discovered. Insects are found in almost every sort of habitat, from deserts to lakes, and from the soil to the air. The only place which insects have been unable to colonize successfully is the oceans, but they make up for this by their abundance elsewhere. Insects vary enormously in their general shape as well as in their size. They range from the microscopic to beetles the size of a large mouse.

Despite the enormous variety of insect life, they all have certain features in common. Like many of their invertebrate relatives, insects have an external skeleton called an exoskeleton which provides support and protection. The bodies of adult insects are divided into three parts: the head, the thorax and the abdomen, and on the middle part are found three pairs of jointed legs.

Insect Lives

Perhaps the most striking feature of insects is their ability to fly. It is the conquest of the air which has helped insects to become so successful. Some insects, such as beetles, are relatively cumbersome in flight and can cover only short distances. Others, however, such as dragonflies, spend virtually all the hours of daylight on the wing. Their mastery of the air, and their excellent vision, allow them to catch even the speediest of airborne prey.

The wings of many butterflies are extremely colourful and are used for a variety of purposes such as display, defence and camouflage, in addition to their use in flight.

Insects eat many different types of food. Many, like the antlion larva above, are carnivores while others eat only plant material. Some insects even eat plants at one stage in their life and animals in another. Others are scavengers, or attack man's clothes, books and carpets. Even more extraordinarily some insects, such as certain moths, do not feed at all as adults.

Above: The antlion is a curious insect which is found in dry, sandy soils. The larva is a fierce carnivore with a liking for ants, but it is so slow and cumbersome that it has to use cunning means to catch its food. Instead of chasing its prey, the antlion larva buries itself in the sand and digs a pit. Any unfortunate ant which falls over the edge of the pit slowly but surely slides down into the jaws of the waiting larva.

Insects have well-developed senses that tell them everything they need to know about their surroundings. Unlike our own eyes, the 'compound' eyes of insects are composed of up to 25,000 separate chambers each with a small lens. Although giving

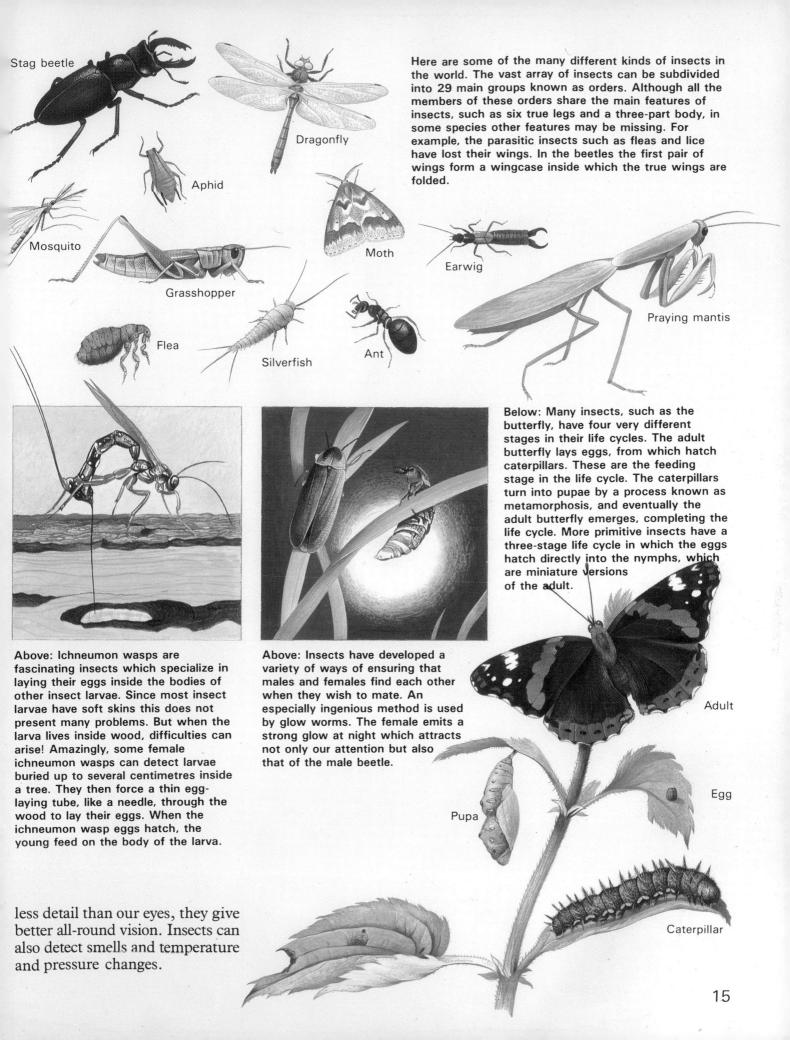

Stag beetle

Dragonfly

Aphid

Here are some of the many different kinds of insects in the world. The vast array of insects can be subdivided into 29 main groups known as orders. Although all the members of these orders share the main features of insects, such as six true legs and a three-part body, in some species other features may be missing. For example, the parasitic insects such as fleas and lice have lost their wings. In the beetles the first pair of wings form a wingcase inside which the true wings are folded.

Mosquito

Moth

Earwig

Grasshopper

Praying mantis

Flea

Silverfish

Ant

Below: Many insects, such as the butterfly, have four very different stages in their life cycles. The adult butterfly lays eggs, from which hatch caterpillars. These are the feeding stage in the life cycle. The caterpillars turn into pupae by a process known as metamorphosis, and eventually the adult butterfly emerges, completing the life cycle. More primitive insects have a three-stage life cycle in which the eggs hatch directly into the nymphs, which are miniature versions of the adult.

Above: Ichneumon wasps are fascinating insects which specialize in laying their eggs inside the bodies of other insect larvae. Since most insect larvae have soft skins this does not present many problems. But when the larva lives inside wood, difficulties can arise! Amazingly, some female ichneumon wasps can detect larvae buried up to several centimetres inside a tree. They then force a thin egg-laying tube, like a needle, through the wood to lay their eggs. When the ichneumon wasp eggs hatch, the young feed on the body of the larva.

Above: Insects have developed a variety of ways of ensuring that males and females find each other when they wish to mate. An especially ingenious method is used by glow worms. The female emits a strong glow at night which attracts not only our attention but also that of the male beetle.

Adult

Egg

Pupa

Caterpillar

less detail than our eyes, they give better all-round vision. Insects can also detect smells and temperature and pressure changes.

Social Insects

Most insects lead independent lives, coming together with others of their kind only for mating. However, some insects can only survive in complex societies. On their own they would soon die.

In insect societies the whole colony is often based on one breeding female, called a queen. In most cases, all the other members of the society are her offspring. There is usually a well-defined division of labour, with different types of colony members produced for different tasks. This is called a caste system. For example, some members of the colony will defend it, and they have large, aggressive mouthparts. Others may be concerned with collection of food and repairing the nest or hive, and may have chewing mouthparts.

In the ants and termites, the solitary queen is often little more than an egg-laying machine. She devotes all her life to laying eggs but cannot defend or feed herself.

Ants

Ants are interesting social insects which live in large colonies either underground or in loose mounds. Their homes contain a complex system of tunnels and galleries. Ant societies contain three castes: the males, fertile females which become queens, and workers. In the summer, many ants produce wings and fly about looking for mates. These flights are called swarming flights. After mating the fertilized female sheds her wings and searches for a site to start a new colony.

Above: Bees chew bark to make papery nests. These are sometimes built in crevices or suspended from branches. Workers collect pollen to make wax chambers for their young, and nectar to make honey.

Below: Some ants build large mounds of twigs and other plant material. These contain runs and galleries in which the ants live. Many species of ants have a special relationship with aphids. They collect honeydew from the aphids and in return protect them from predators.

Honey Bees

Honey bees are social insects which man uses to his advantage. In the wild, honey bees nest in cavities, but they take readily to artificial hives. Here their honey can be collected without harming the bees.

There are three castes in a honey bee society. At the centre of the colony is the large queen. She is fertile and lays eggs throughout her life, although she only mates once. The next caste is the drones. These are male bees. Their function is to mate with the queen, and they take no part in the running of the hive. The third caste is the workers, which make up most of the bees in the hive. Like the queen, they are female, but they are sterile. As their name suggests, they do most of the work, gathering pollen, making honey and defending the hive with their stings.

Honey bees show many interesting types of behaviour. In hot weather, they fan the entrance to the hive with their wings to produce a draught. The workers also perform elaborate 'dances' which tell other hive members the directions to the best food.

Termites

Termite mounds, like the ones shown at the bottom of this page, are a conspicuous feature of the African Plains, and are common throughout the tropics. These impressive structures may be up to 6 metres tall. Many are made of cemented soil and so they are virtually impregnable.

Termite society is rather different from those of ants, bees and wasps. There are four castes rather than three. A colony is started after winged males and females swarm. When a pair have settled, they shed their wings and the female becomes the queen of the new colony. She becomes grotesquely enlarged and lays more than 10,000 eggs a day when she is mature. The male is also important because he has to fertilize the queen several times throughout her life.

The soldiers are armed with a huge set of jaws with which to defend the mound from attackers. The fourth caste is the workers, who gather the wood which is the main food for termites. They have special bacteria in their intestines which help them digest it.

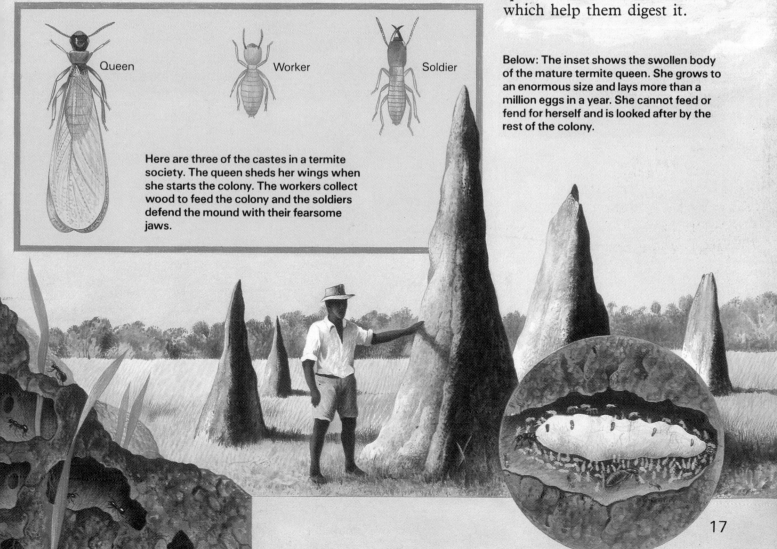

Queen   Worker   Soldier

Here are three of the castes in a termite society. The queen sheds her wings when she starts the colony. The workers collect wood to feed the colony and the soldiers defend the mound with their fearsome jaws.

Below: The inset shows the swollen body of the mature termite queen. She grows to an enormous size and lays more than a million eggs in a year. She cannot feed or fend for herself and is looked after by the rest of the colony.

Pondlife

Freshwater ponds often teem with life. Colourful displays of flowers grow around their edges, and a wealth of animal life lives below the surface. The animals which dwell there must cope with very different problems from those of their relatives on land. They must be able to move about in the water and find a way of obtaining oxygen for breathing. The pond dwellers also have to cope with extremes of temperature; sunny days can heat the water up, while in winter the water's surface may freeze.

Some of the pond's inhabitants, such as fishes, can only live in water, but others, such as frogs and dragonflies, spend the early part of their lives in water and their adult stages on land, returning to the pond to breed in the spring.

Life in Ponds

The pond is not a simple environment, but is really a mixture of several separate habitats. The aquatic plants and animals have all evolved to live in very precise zones of the pond. Some plants will grow only in the drying mud on the margin of the pond while others, which cannot survive drying out, must be constantly immersed in water. Duckweed likes to drift in the open water while other species, such as water lilies, remain rooted in the mud at the bottom.

It is, however, the animal inhabitants which are most specially adapted to life in the pond. The surface of the water is very important. It is here that oxygen enters the pond from the air. It is the place where some animals move from air to water, and also where light penetrates the waters below. However, it can also be a prison to many land animals which get trapped in its surface film. Not surprisingly, a variety of scavengers live on the surface and pick off the unfortunate animals caught there. Still more scavengers live underneath this surface film, often trapping air on their bodies to keep them buoyant.

Below the surface is the open water, inhabited by newts, fishes and water beetles. These creatures

Heron

Right: This panorama of a pond illustrates some of the creatures which live there. In the water itself, great crested newts and sticklebacks feed on the wealth of insect life present. These in turn sometimes fall victim to the carnivorous great diving beetle. Beneath the surface of the water, many plants grow, rooted in the muddy bottom. When they flower, they either produce floating flowers, such as those of the water lily, or tall flowering spikes like those of reeds and bulrushes. Many birds are associated with fresh water. Herons patiently stalk fishes in the shallows while coots dive for plant and animal food.

Pondskater

Water lily

Great diving beetle

Pondweed

Caddis larva

Great crested newt

feed on others which hide among the tangled pond weeds, and seldom visit either the surface or the bottom.

On the bottom, where the silt collects and where the remains of dead plants and animals fall, many species such as bloodworms and crustaceans tolerate its inhospitable conditions and find it a safe sanctuary away from the eyes of hungry predators.

In order to obtain the oxygen they require for breathing, many freshwater insects come to the surface to breathe, although some, such as damselfly nymphs, have developed simple gills to help them extract oxygen from the water. Many diving beetles have an ingenious way of breathing. They trap a bubble of air under their wingcases and this acts as a kind of 'aqualung'. But, like its human equivalent, it must be topped up from time to time, so the beetle makes regular visits to the surface.

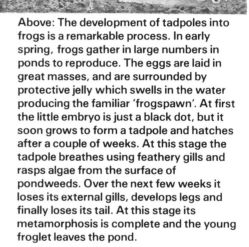

Above: The development of tadpoles into frogs is a remarkable process. In early spring, frogs gather in large numbers in ponds to reproduce. The eggs are laid in great masses, and are surrounded by protective jelly which swells in the water producing the familiar 'frogspawn'. At first the little embryo is just a black dot, but it soon grows to form a tadpole and hatches after a couple of weeks. At this stage the tadpole breathes using feathery gills and rasps algae from the surface of pondweeds. Over the next few weeks it loses its external gills, develops legs and finally loses its tail. At this stage its metamorphosis is complete and the young froglet leaves the pond.

Water plants produce oxygen when they photosynthesize. One little animal named Hydra has found an ingenious way of making use of this. It incorporates small, single-celled green algae between its cells and then 'breathes' the oxygen they produce.

HALFWAY ANIMALS

Frogs, toads and newts belong to a group of animals known as amphibians. They are thought to have evolved from fish ancestors and to have given rise to reptiles. Fishes are almost exclusively aquatic animals, whereas reptiles are almost entirely land dwellers. Amphibians are usually just as much at home in water as they are on land.

When adults, frogs, toads and newts can breathe by taking in oxygen through their skins, but they can also gulp air through their mouths. This enables them to leave the water when they wish. Although some amphibians may spend most of their adult lives away from water, they must all return to the water to breed.

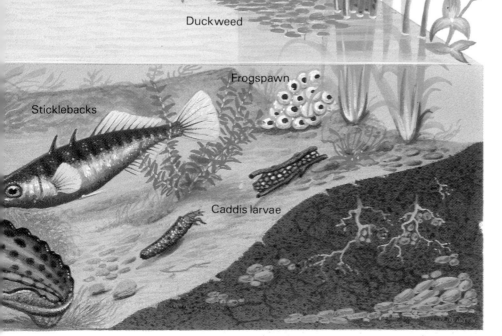

The Seashore

A great variety of interesting and unusual wildlife is to be found on the seashore. In fact, some of the plants and animals of the seashore — such as seaweeds and sea urchins — are found nowhere else.

All the animals and plants of the seashore are extremely hardy, for as well as having to cope with the pounding of the waves they must be able to survive when the tide goes out, leaving them exposed to the drying sun and wind. At this time they are also easy prey for predators, and so must find ways of protecting themselves.

The most common plants of the seashore are seaweeds. Seaweeds belong to a group of plants called algae. The seaweeds grow on the beach according to their ability to withstand exposure when the tide is out.

The most curious seashore plants are the lichens. Some resemble patches of tar stuck to the rocks. Others look like little orange crusty patches.

Types of Seashore

There are several different kinds of seashore. Rocky shores are usually richest in wildlife. The rocks provide good anchorage for the seaweeds, and the crevices offer a safe haven for snails, worms, crabs and other creatures. Many of the snails' relatives, such as limpets and mussels, clamp themselves to the rocks. Countless barnacles, related to crabs and prawns, also cover many of the rocks.

In the rockpools starfishes, anemones and fishes lurk, safe from the wind and sun.

Sandy shores are more difficult places for wildlife to survive. There is little shelter for animals, and so they must burrow beneath the sand to find a moist, secure place to live. Lugworms, fanworms and a great variety of bivalves such as cockles, razorshells and tellins are to be found living in the sand.

Even more harsh environments are shingle beaches. The relentless, grinding action of the pebbles would crush most animals. Therefore the only living things here are specially adapted flowering plants like sea kale.

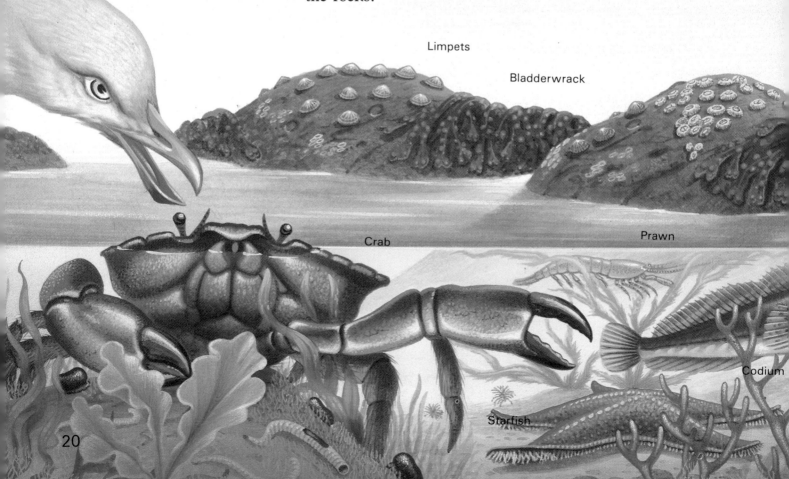

Gull

Limpets

Bladderwrack

Crab

Prawn

Codium

Starfish

Pelican's foot

Razor shell

Whelk

Necklace shell

Cockle

Wedge shell

Tern

Above: You will often find shells such as these on beaches. These shells once belonged to animals called molluscs, one of the commonest groups of creatures on the seashore. Other common molluscs include periwinkles and limpets.

Below: Seashores, particularly sheltered rocky shores, teem with animal and plant life. Some creatures live attached to the rocks themselves, while others seek refuge in rockpools or under the sand. Birds such as gulls and waders patrol the shore, looking for food.

ADAPTING TO LIFE ON THE SEASHORE

Some of the seashore animals have strong shells into which they can retreat at low tide, remaining moist and secure until the tide returns. Others are masters of camouflage; certain crabs and worms look like the seaweed in which they hide. The fronds of the seaweed also help to keep the creatures moist.

The seaweeds attach themselves to rocks by means of a root-like structure called a holdfast. They also have soft, slippery stems and fronds which enable them to sway in the currents and avoid becoming damaged. Some species, like bladderwrack, have special air bubbles in their fronds, which help them to float.

Barnacles

Lichen

Mussels

Blenny

Fan worm

Anemone

Sea cucumber

Life in the Seas

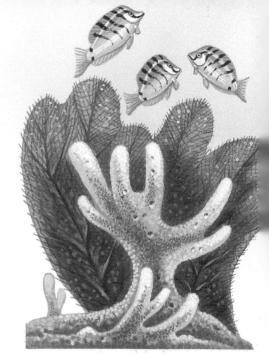

The seas and oceans cover nearly three-quarters of the world's surface, and are extremely rich and varied habitats. From the shallowest coastal waters to the huge expanses of the open ocean, and from the icy polar waters to the tropical seas, they literally teem with life.

Shallow Seas

In the shallow coastal waters we often find plants and animals similar to those found on the seashore, such as seaweeds, crabs, snails, bivalves (molluscs with hinged shells), starfishes and many other familiar creatures such as seals and sea lions.

In the warmer parts of the world the shallow waters are often the home of corals. These tiny creatures, related to anemones, build chalky homes around themselves. Eventually these may extend for many kilometres. Coral reefs are fascinating places in which fishes, starfishes, sea urchins and anemones and other creatures all live together in a bewildering array of colours and shapes.

Above: These dazzling clown fish are among the many colourful species which inhabit coral reefs. The world's biggest coral reef is the Great Barrier Reef, extending for 2012 kilometres along the north-eastern coast of Australia.

Below: Most sharks are fearsome predators of the sea, although a few species eat only plankton. Dolphins and porpoises are kinds of whale. Whales are mammals which spend all their lives in the sea. Many seabirds feed on fishes which they catch near the surface.

Tern

Shark

Dolphin

Open Oceans

The smallest forms of life in the open sea are the plankton. These are tiny, microscopic plants and animals which float near the surface. They provide food for many of the other species of animal living in the sea. Even some of the huge whales and sharks live just on a diet of plankton. Most of the sharks, however, are fierce predators of other animals, particularly the huge shoals of fishes which roam the oceans. Species such as the hammerhead and the great white shark are even feared by man, for attacks on humans are not uncommon in waters in which they are found.

Turtles and sea snakes are reptiles frequently encountered in the open sea. Turtles are generally found in warmer waters. They spend most of their lives at sea, only hauling themselves on to beaches at night to lay their eggs in the sand. As soon as they hatch, the baby turtles must scuttle back down the beach to return to the safety of the sea.

Sea snakes are highly venomous, and about 50 species are known to inhabit the sea, mainly in the waters of the Indo-Pacific region. They feed on small fishes.

Deep Sea

In the gloom of the deep sea, where light never reaches, some of the most bizarre creatures are to be found. These include giant squids, prawns and angler fishes.

Portuguese man o'war

Jellyfish

Above: Jellyfishes and the Portuguese man o'war drift in the open oceans. They catch fishes and other small creatures, using their trailing tentacles which are armed with powerful stinging cells.

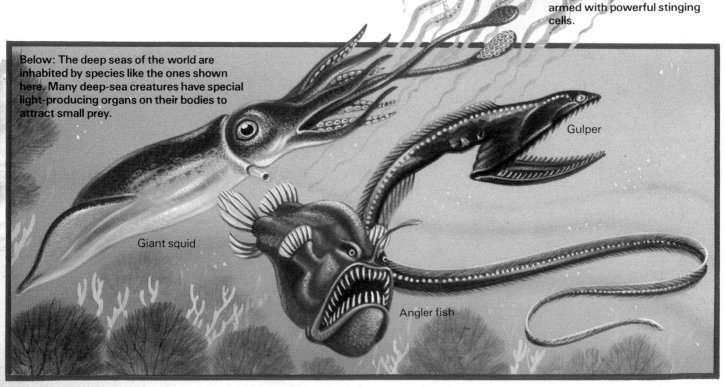

Below: The deep seas of the world are inhabited by species like the ones shown here. Many deep-sea creatures have special light-producing organs on their bodies to attract small prey.

Giant squid

Gulper

Angler fish

The Reptilian World

Reptiles are scaly, cold-blooded vertebrate animals which lay eggs with hard, protective shells. The reptiles descended from amphibians 300 million years ago. Today, reptiles are found mainly in the warmer parts of the world.

Many millions of years ago, there were many more kinds of reptiles on the earth than there are today. During the period in the earth's history known as the Mesozoic Era, huge reptiles roamed over many continents. Other reptiles conquered the sea and air. About 70 million years ago many reptiles died out, however.

Above: The anaconda is a large snake from South America which kills its prey by constriction or squeezing, before swallowing it whole. The anaconda is also found in rivers.

Left: A cobra rears up in this position before striking at its prey.

Below: Snakes can open their mouths extremely wide. This is how they are able to swallow big prey.

Living Reptiles

The biggest group of living reptiles is the Squamata. These include the snakes and lizards. Snakes are reptiles which have lost the use of their legs over the course of evolution. They move along by means of special movements of their muscular bodies, and they also use their scales to help obtain a grip as they move. A few species swim in the sea.

All snakes are predators, feeding on many different kinds of animal food from eggs to creatures as big as pigs. Some snakes kill their prey before eating it by first squeezing it to death. To do this they quickly surprise their victim and wrap their coils tightly around it. Smaller prey is often swallowed alive. Snakes such as adders, cobras and rattlesnakes first inject their prey with a venom before swallowing it.

Lizards have adapted to many different ways of life. They are also predators but, unlike the snakes, only two species are venomous. The biggest lizard is the Komodo dragon of Borneo. This huge creature measures 3 metres in length. It eats large prey. Most lizards, however, feed on small mammals and birds, as well as on insects and other invertebrates.

The Crocodilia forms the second group of living reptiles. This group includes the crocodiles, caimans, alligators and the gharial. Members of the Crocodilia look very much like their ancestors which existed when reptiles ruled the earth.

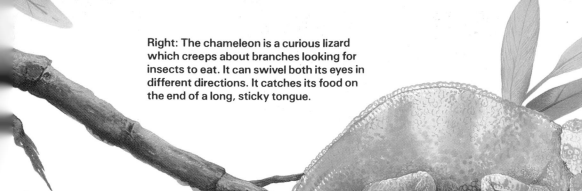

Right: The chameleon is a curious lizard which creeps about branches looking for insects to eat. It can swivel both its eyes in different directions. It catches its food on the end of a long, sticky tongue.

Below: The heads of three different crocodilians.

Alligator

Crocodile

Caiman

Below: The giant tortoise of the Galapagos Islands is big enough for a man to ride. A common tortoise is shown by its side.

Crocodilians look like huge, armour-plated lizards. They are all adapted to a life spent in water, where they lurk partly submerged beneath the surface waiting for prey. Sometimes they will snatch animals that come to the water's edge to drink. At night they may leave the water to sleep on a sandbank.

The tails of crocodilians are specially flattened for swimming, and the nostrils are placed high on the snout, enabling them to breathe even when lying partly submerged in water.

Crocodilians are found in many parts of the world. They live in the fresh waters of tropical Asia, Africa, Australia and America. One species, the estuarine crocodile, is found in the estuaries of rivers in parts of Asia and Australia. It also swims out to sea.

The most unusual-looking crocodilian is the gharial of India. It has long, thin jaws armed with sharp teeth. Despite its fearsome appearance, however, it catches nothing bigger than fishes.

The Chelonia comprise the tortoises, terrapins and turtles. The chelonians carry on their back a bony shield, and their underbodies are protected by a large, flat, bony plate. When danger threatens these animals can pull their heads and limbs inside their protective armour. Unlike other reptiles, chelonians do not possess teeth, but they have sharp, bony beaks. Also, unlike other reptiles, some chelonians are herbivorous.

Although there are exceptions, most tortoises are land-living creatures, most terrapins live in fresh water, and turtles live in the sea.

The last group of living reptiles is the Rhynchocephalia. Only one living member of this group exists. This animal is called the tuatara. It lives on remote islands near New Zealand, and looks rather like a lizard with spines on its back. It often shares a burrow with a bird, the Manx shearwater.

Birdlife

It would be impossible to mistake a bird for any other animal, for only birds possess feathers. It is feathers which have given birds mastery of the air.

There are nearly 9,000 species of birds throughout the world today, living in every sort of habitat from the seashore to the jungle. The smallest birds are the brilliantly coloured hummingbirds, whose nests are no bigger than a thimble. At the other end of the scale is the ostrich, a flightless bird standing 2.5 metres high.

Birds have adapted to feed on all manner of food. There are some species, the birds of prey, which hunt other animals. Others eat seeds and fruit. A few feed on nothing but insects. Hummingbirds hover over flowers and suck up nectar.

Above: The eagle has a sharp, flesh-tearing beak.

Above: Ducks have wide, flat beaks for sifting mud.

Bird Flight

The ability to fly is the key to the great success of birds. Flight has enabled birds to travel huge distances in search of new territories; to travel from continent to continent during migration; and it has allowed them to escape from their enemies when danger threatens.

For successful flight birds must have lightweight, streamlined bodies. Bird bones are hollow, but specially strengthened, and the feathers help to give them a smooth shape in the air. Lift and motion through the air is provided by the feathers on the wings. The tail is used for steering. Birds which spend hours soaring over oceans have long, narrow wings. Birds which fly fast have sickle-shaped wings. Birds which must fly between the trees have shorter, powerful wings.

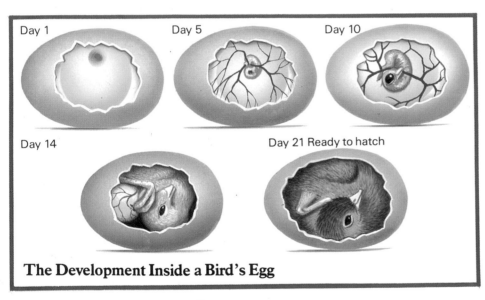

Day 1   Day 5   Day 10

Day 14   Day 21 Ready to hatch

The Development Inside a Bird's Egg

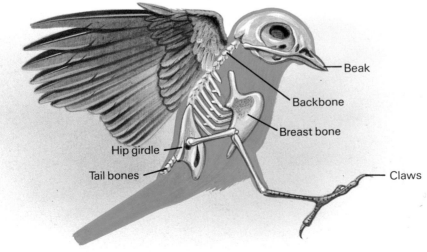

Beak

Backbone

Breast bone

Hip girdle

Tail bones

Claws

Left: This is how the skeleton is arranged inside a typical bird such as a crow.

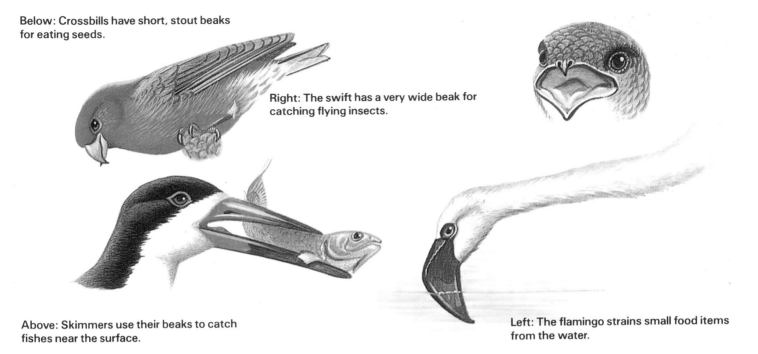

Below: Crossbills have short, stout beaks for eating seeds.

Right: The swift has a very wide beak for catching flying insects.

Above: Skimmers use their beaks to catch fishes near the surface.

Left: The flamingo strains small food items from the water.

Birds and their Young

Many animals build a nest in which to rear their young in safety, but the most familiar of these are birds' nests. Not all birds build nests, however. Some species simply lay their eggs on the ground. The cuckoo is an unusual bird which lays its eggs in the nest of another species.

Before nesting begins, most birds choose a territory and defend it against rivals. The number of eggs laid by the female depends on the species. It may be just one, or as many as 20. Once hatched, the young chicks are fed by their parents until they are big enough to fend for themselves. Most chicks are blind and helpless at birth, but the chicks of waterbirds are born fully feathered and can swim straight away.

Great crested grebes have an elaborate courtship display known as a mating dance.

Right: Many birds, like this whip-poor-will, use their plumage for concealment.

27

Apes and Monkeys

Apes and monkeys, together with the tree shrews, lemurs, lorises and bush-babies, make up the group of animals known as the primates. In many ways primates are extremely interesting creatures, because man is also a primate. Many monkeys and apes spend their lives in the safety of the treetops. A few, however, have returned to live a life on the ground. Ground-dwelling species include the baboon, the gorilla and, of course, man himself.

    Apes and monkeys are intelligent creatures. They have relatively large brains, and forward-facing eyes which help them to judge distances well. Their hands and feet are designed to help them grip branches as they leap from tree to tree. They often live together in well-organized family groups.

Gibbon

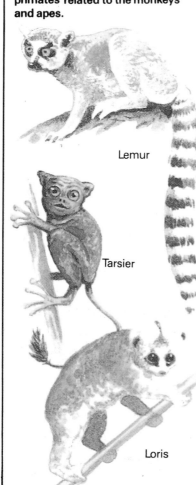

These three animals are primitive primates related to the monkeys and apes.

Lemur

Tarsier

Loris

Below: Baboons are large, African, dog-like monkeys which live mainly on the ground. They live in family groups and eat all kinds of food. They defend themselves fiercely if attacked.

Above: Gibbons are apes with very long arms. They swing through the trees with great ease, but can also run along branches. They live in Asian forests and feed mainly on fruit.

Baboon

Gorilla

Orang-utan

Chimpanzee

Spider monkey

Above: Chimpanzees are highly intelligent apes which spend part of their lives in the treetops of African forests and part on the ground. They can use their hands in a way very similar to us.

Right: Spider monkeys are extremely agile climbers which can also use their tails to hang on to branches.

Below left: Mandrills are forest-dwelling baboons which live in Africa.

Above: The orang-utan is an ape which lives in Borneo and Sumatra.

Left: Despite their huge size and fierce appearance, gorillas are shy, plant-eating apes.

Mandrill

Monkeys

Monkeys are divided into two groups: those that live in places like South America, and those that live in Africa, India and Asia. Some monkeys are active during the day, where they search for fruit, leaves, insects or other small animals to eat. Others come out only at night, when their strange calls fill the warm night air.

Apes

There are ten species of apes, all of which live in the tropical forests of Africa and Asia. One group, which includes the gorilla, orang-utan and chimpanzee, is known as the 'great apes'. Apes are the group of primates most closely related to man.

How Animals Communicate

Animals communicate with each other for several reasons. Between members of the same species they may communicate in order to find a mate in the breeding season, or to warn other rivals that they have chosen a particular place as their territory. Watch a bird such as a robin. In the breeding season it will fly from tree to tree, or perhaps perch on a fence, and each time it lands it will sing. In fact, what it is really doing is flying around the boundaries of its territory, telling other robins to keep out.

The fiddler crab communicates by means of 'hand signals'. When the male wishes to attract a female, it sits on the sand and beckons the female with a wave of one of its pincers, which is specially enlarged.

Above: Songbirds, like the American robin shown here, sing to warn other birds that they have chosen a territory, and to attract a mate.

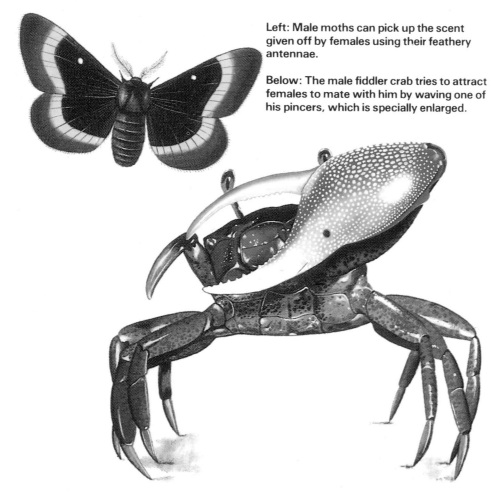

Left: Male moths can pick up the scent given off by females using their feathery antennae.

Below: The male fiddler crab tries to attract females to mate with him by waving one of his pincers, which is specially enlarged.

Whales swimming through the vast oceans of the world communicate by sound. Scientists have often recorded the mournful calls of the humpback whale, which can carry over hundreds of kilometres.

Animals often tell each other about the presence of food, or warn each other of possible danger. Sometimes one bird in a feeding flock will alert the others to a source of food and the rest of the flock will quickly gather to feed. In order to survive, different species of animals have learned to heed each other's warnings. The frantic clap of wings made by a pigeon alarmed in a wood is also a signal to other animals such as squirrels and deer that danger is present. And when lions come to feed at an African waterhole the first grazing animal to spot the danger quickly alerts the others, as zebra, wildebeest, gazelles and even elephants all run to safety.

Many animals are poisonous, and this prevents them being eaten

Right: Timber wolves live in forests and snow-covered wastes. They communicate to other members of the pack by means of special calls. This helps to keep the pack together, even at night.

by predators. Animals which are poisonous, or which are highly venomous, advertise this fact by having brightly coloured bodies. Coral snakes, arrow-poison frogs, ladybirds, kingfishers and wasps are just a few of the many animals which tell other animals that they are poisonous. Sometimes other harmless animals mimic these poisonous species in the hope that they, too, will be left alone by predators.

Right: The skins of arrow-poison frogs contain a very powerful poison, and their brightly coloured bodies warn predators that they are poisonous. The African elephant gives warning to its enemies by drawing its ears forward in a threat display. The caterpillar of the elephant hawkmoth is harmless, but tries to alarm would-be predators by rearing up and showing its eye spots.

THE BEE DANCE

One of the most fascinating examples of communication is to be found among honey bees. Hive members returning from a foray tell other bees about the location of good sources of food, by performing a kind of dance. The speed and direction of the dance indicate the position of the food very accurately. If the food is within 100 metres or so the bee performs a round dance — quick circular motions made first in one direction and then the other. If the food is further away she performs a waggle dance — a figure-of-eight performed while waggling her abdomen. The angle at which she performs the dance tells other bees about the direction of the food.

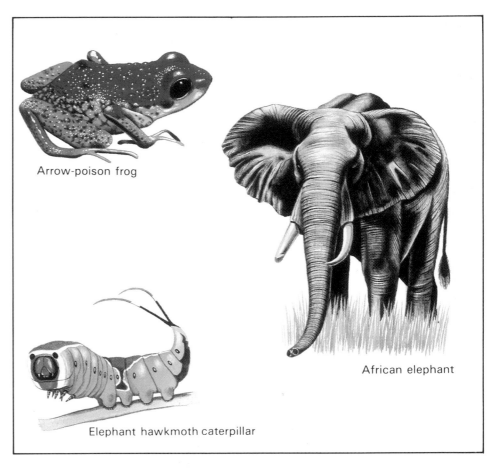

Arrow-poison frog

African elephant

Elephant hawkmoth caterpillar

Right: Honey bees returning to their hive after a food foray inform other hive members about the location of food, by performing a sort of dance.

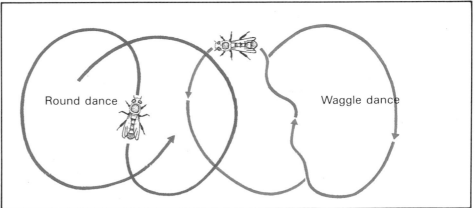

Round dance

Waggle dance

Attack and Defence

For many animals, life in the wild is harsh. Most grazing (plant-eating) animals are preyed upon by meat eaters. Even animals which eat other creatures may themselves become a meal for a bigger predator.

Animals which attack others in order to eat them use many different methods to catch their prey, and an array of weapons with which to overpower them. For example, large predatory mammals such as lions, tigers and cheetahs have powerful limbs, and jaws armed with sharp teeth. Most big cats chase their prey before knocking it to the ground with a blow from their paws. Then they bite the victim in the neck, quickly killing it.

Sometimes animals attack each other for reasons other than to catch food. During the mating season particularly, animals will fight, occasionally to the death, over a mate or a territory.

Above: The trapdoor spider lies cunningly concealed in a trap, waiting for prey. As soon as a likely meal passes, the spider rushes out and overpowers its victim by injecting it with a deadly venom.

Above: The peregrine (left) dives from the air on to its victim. It can fly at such great speed that few birds can escape it. The polar bear (right) catches seals which emerge from ice holes to obtain air.

Tadpole

Dragonfly larva

Left: Dragonfly larvae have special jaws called a mask with which they grab their prey.

Left: Lions hunt their prey together. Some of the lions chase the prey to where other lions are lying in wait for them.

There are many ways in which animals try to avoid being eaten. Some animals are poisonous or distasteful to eat, and warn would-be predators of this fact by wearing bright 'warning colours'. Others are just too big to be eaten; no predator could attack and kill a fully grown rhinoceros or elephant.

Some creatures are quite able to look after themselves. Many types of antelope have sharp horns which can cause severe wounds to unwary predators. Others live in a herd, and are able to run fast. Quite often the predator will single out the weak or old members of the herd and leave the stronger members to escape.

Many creatures, particularly insects, rely on camouflage or a secretive way of life to avoid being spotted by predators.

Mountain hare (summer)

Mountain hare (winter)

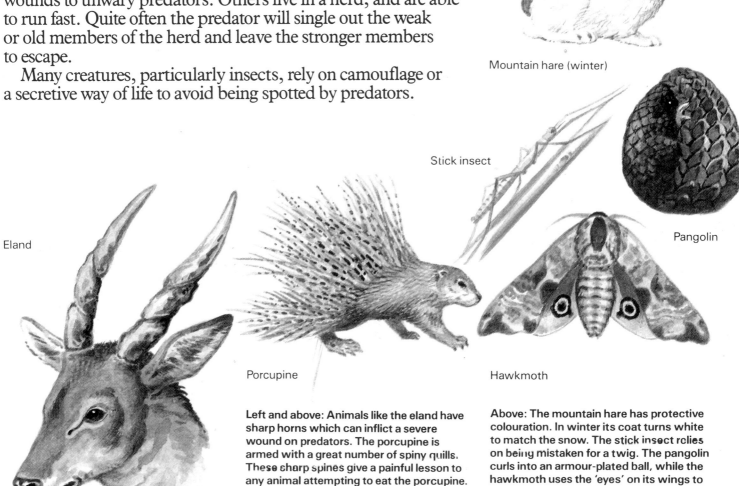

Stick insect

Pangolin

Eland

Porcupine

Hawkmoth

Left and above: Animals like the eland have sharp horns which can inflict a severe wound on predators. The porcupine is armed with a great number of spiny quills. These sharp spines give a painful lesson to any animal attempting to eat the porcupine.

Above: The mountain hare has protective colouration. In winter its coat turns white to match the snow. The stick insect relies on being mistaken for a twig. The pangolin curls into an armour-plated ball, while the hawkmoth uses the 'eyes' on its wings to alarm would-be predators.

33

Animals and their Young

Animals must reproduce in order that each species can continue. The simplest animals, like the amoeba, reproduce by simply splitting into two. Most animals, however, reproduce by means of a male and female mating together.

For many animals, the first task in reproduction is to find a safe place to lay their eggs or give birth to their young. In the insect world, many species lay their eggs in holes or crevices, or glued safely to the underside of leaves away from the eyes of predators. Some insects, for example some kinds of wasps, even put in a supply of food ready for the young to eat when they hatch.

Other species of animals may have to fend for themselves as soon as they are born.

Above: Many species of snakes coil themselves around their eggs. This helps to protect the eggs from predators, but also keeps the eggs warm during incubation.

Below: Mammals, like the opossum shown here, feed their young with milk, produced in the mammary glands of the female.

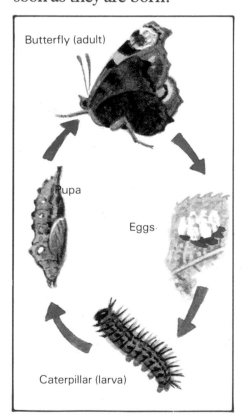

Above: Many insects undergo a four-stage life cycle. The adult lays eggs which hatch into larvae. The larvae feed and grow, and turn into pupae. From the pupae emerge new adults.

Right: A reed bunting feeding its chicks at the nest.

Many kinds of birds build nests in which to lay their eggs and rear their young. During spring, both parents will often work ceaselessly hour after hour, building an elaborate nest of twigs, grass, leaves and down so that their chicks will hatch safe from enemies such as snakes or other birds.

Some animals display a remarkable degree of parental care towards their young. We often think of crocodiles as ferocious animals but, as soon as the young hatch from their eggs, the mother crocodile carries her babies gently in her mouth to a safe place.

Once born, the job of finding food begins. Although many creatures must find food for themselves when they are born, most of the more advanced animals, such as birds and mammals, rely on their parents to provide nourishment for them until they have grown big enough to feed themselves.

Above: Scorpions show a remarkable form of parental care. When the young have hatched, they climb on to their parents' back and are carried about, safe from danger.

Below: Many animals, like these brown bear cubs, are taught how to hunt by their parents. Play fighting also helps them to fend for themselves in the wild. The mother watches over the cubs while they play.

Animals on the Move

Each year many animals make long journeys in search of food, shelter from harsh weather or a place to breed. These journeys are called migrations. Among the best-known migrations are the annual journeys from Europe to Africa made by cuckoos, swallows, warblers and many other birds.

Many animals live in parts of the world where the climate changes throughout the year. In the temperate zones these changes are regular and are called seasons, although in the tropics there is little change from one month to the next. As the seasons change the conditions can become less suitable for feeding or breeding; some animals can cope with these changes, perhaps by hibernating, but others overcome the threat of harsh conditions by moving to more favourable areas.

Insect Migration

We normally think of migration as being undertaken only by larger animals, but many insects, especially some butterflies, undergo migrations as lengthy as those carried out by birds and mammals.

The red admiral is a colourful butterfly which is found in north Africa and the Mediterranean. Each spring, however, some of them move northwards into Europe and breed as far north as England and Scandinavia. The following autumn, a few of the new generation fly south to escape the onset of the cold weather. Although many perish on the way, some survive the return journey — an impressive feat for an insect.

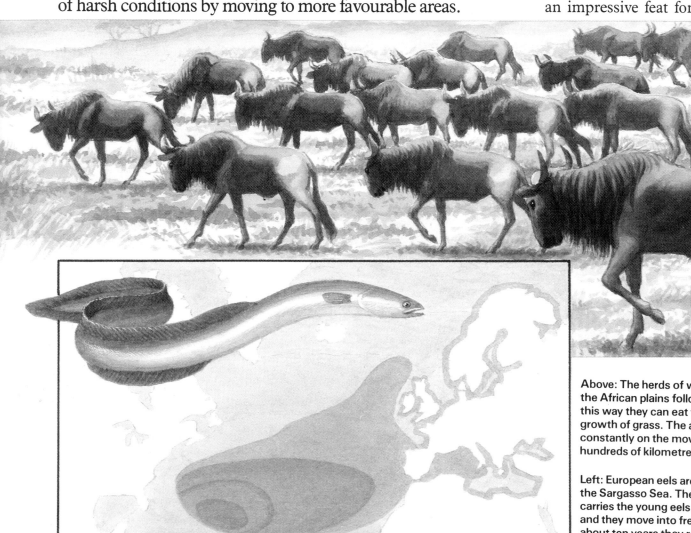

Above: The herds of wildebeest on the African plains follow the rains. In this way they can eat the new growth of grass. The animals are constantly on the move, covering hundreds of kilometres a year.

Left: European eels are spawned in the Sargasso Sea. The Gulf Stream carries the young eels to our shores and they move into fresh water. After about ten years they return to the sea to breed.

Above: In some years lemming numbers reach plague proportions. To escape the overcrowding many go on mass migration. At this time predators such as snowy owls and foxes benefit from their abundance.

Below: Bird migrations often involve vast distances and require spectacular navigational skills. Many migrate from northern regions to more temperate areas. Some, like arctic terns, cross to the southern hemisphere for the winter.

Canada goose

Arctic warbler

Cuckoo

Golden plover

Arctic tern

Migration of Larger Animals

Both marine mammals as well as land-living species undergo migrations. Seals leave their breeding grounds in spring, and return to warmer seas to spend the winter. When feeding becomes poor many mammals just keep moving until they find better conditions. Herds of animals in Africa follow the rains, grazing the fresh growth of grass that follows. Some reptiles also migrate. Marine turtles haul themselves on to the same beach every year to lay their eggs.

The movements of birds have evolved to become extremely predictable, and they often follow distinct routes over long distances. The arctic tern is famous for its travels from its breeding grounds in the arctic to its wintering area in the antarctic. In its travels it covers over 32,000 kilometres a year, and probably over 160,000 kilometres in its lifetime. As well as travelling further in its life than most other living creatures it also sees more daylight than species which remain in one area.

Nocturnal Life

When darkness falls over the town and countryside, another world comes to life — the world of nocturnal plants and animals. The animals which had been active during the day seek safe places to shelter for the night, and other creatures take their place.

When the sun goes down the temperature drops, and moisture forms on the ground and in the air. These are ideal conditions for the small creatures which thrive in a damp environment. Earthworms, insects, spiders, centipedes and other small invertebrates creep from their hiding places to find food or to mate.

In the darkness other, larger creatures feel safe, too, and leave their burrows to hunt. Mice and voles search for insects, seeds and other food items. They in turn fall prey to the hunters of the night — the predatory animals such as foxes, stoats and owls. Larger creatures such as deer leave the safety of the woodland to graze in the clearings.

Most nocturnal animals are specially adapted for their night-time existence. Badgers and deer have a well-developed sense of smell, for instance. Deer also have acute hearing. Moths can detect the scent given off by females from great distances. Owls swoop down on their prey without warning, for their wings make scarcely a sound as they beat.

Animal Architects

When we visit a cathedral we marvel at the skill of the men who constructed it. But if we consider the building feats achieved by some animals, often working entirely alone, some of these are equally amazing.

Animals build for similar reasons to people; to make a shelter from the elements, protection for themselves or their young, or in order to catch food. Animal shelters and homes range from the little tubes of caddis larvae, to the often complex nests which birds build for their eggs and young.

Some animal constructions are quite small, and are designed to accommodate only their makers. Others, such as termite mounds, are enormous, and provide a home for thousands of individuals. Building material also varies. Some animals use materials they gather from their surroundings, and others produce the building material themselves. Spiders, for instance, make their webs from the silk which they spin inside their own bodies.

Above: The Great Barrier Reef is the only structure built by animals which can be seen from space. It was constructed by tiny marine organisms called coral polyps, like the ones seen here, which encase themselves in a tough chalky shell.

Nests

Birds are among the most familiar of animal architects. At the start of each breeding season, many species of birds build a nest in which to lay their eggs and rear their young. Many nests are quite simple structures consisting of interwoven twigs or grass stems. Sometimes these are neatly arranged, and in other species they are a jumbled mass of material. Often these nests are placed in the fork of a tree or in a crevice, giving the nest support.

Nests are usually built from material which the birds gather close by. This makes the nest quick to build, as well as helping it blend into the surroundings. The long-tailed tit's nest is particularly difficult to spot, since the birds use a mixture of lichens, spider's silk and dry grass.

Below: Many spiders produce sticky silk which they spin into beautiful but deadly webs. These trap flying insects which the spider quickly bites and paralyses. The victim is then wrapped in silk, ready for eating later.

Other Homes

The larvae of the caddis fly are also skilled architects. These soft-bodied freshwater insects protect themselves by building tough tubes in which to live. Each species has its own favourite building material; some use plant leaves, others use sand or snail shells. The tube is open at one end, and the larvae drag themselves around using their front legs.

Termites are tropical insects which live in large colonies. Their mounds, which are usually made from soil, are very strong. They can also become very large, often exceeding 6 metres in height. This feat is all the more remarkable when you consider that the animals which built them were less than 1 centimetre long.

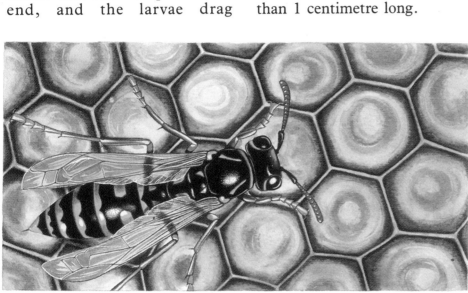

Above: Many wasps are social insects which build papery nests in which to rear their young. They construct layers of hexagonal-shaped chambers in which the eggs are laid and the young wasp larvae grow.

Below: The beaver lodge is a remarkable structure of twigs and logs with its own underwater entrance. Built on a river, the beaver constructs a dam to raise the water level around the lodge.

Above: Weavers are birds which build nests together in thorn bushes. The nests are very carefully woven from grass, and often have long entrances designed to prevent predators getting in.

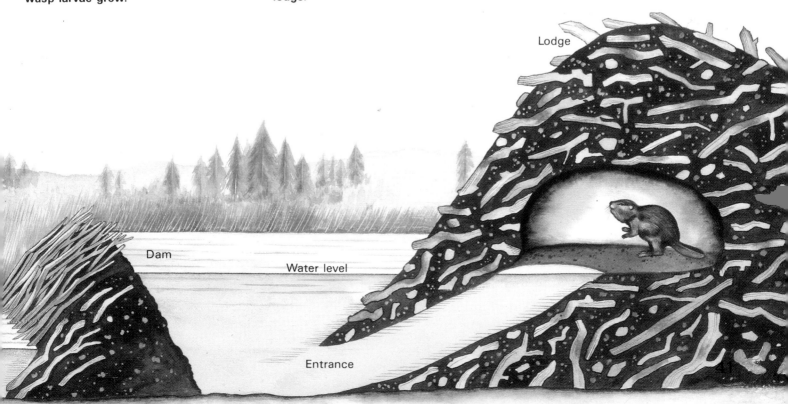

Lodge

Dam

Water level

Entrance

Animal Curiosities

Throughout the Animal Kingdom there is an incredible array of sizes, shapes, colours and behaviour. At first glance some of these animals may seem particularly strange, but in nature there is always a good reason for any peculiarity. What, to our eyes, may seem strange, is in fact essential for an animal's survival in its chosen environment. The more we study nature the more we realize that there is no 'ordinary' animal. Each species has evolved its own shape, colour and behaviour to ensure its survival.

Nevertheless, there are some animals whose appearance and life styles almost defy the imagination. There are fishes that fly and others that walk on dry land, mammals that can fly in complete darkness, spiders that spin webs under water and many more extraordinary creatures.

Below: Many animals hide from predators, but not so the colourful sea slug which actually advertises its presence. The bright colours warn predators of its unpleasant taste.

Unusual Spiders

Many spiders spin silk webs to catch their prey. As if this extraordinary feat were not enough, some use their silk in even more unusual ways. For example, the spitting spider does as its name suggests; it spits silk over its prey until it is so entangled that it cannot escape.

The purse web spider does not spin an ordinary web at all. Instead, it lives under ground in a silken tube strengthened with plant fibres. Part of the tube lies on the ground, however, and when a passing insect crawls over its surface, the spider rushes up the tube and grabs the victim through the tube. Needless to say, the tube needs considerable repair after this!

Below left: The water spider spends its life under water, constructing air-bells in which to live and lay its eggs.

Below right: The crab spider pretends to be the inside of a flower. When an insect lands, it is grabbed by the waiting spider.

Odd-shaped Eggs

Bird's eggs are sometimes brightly coloured and sometimes camouflaged to escape the attention of predators, but nearly all eggs are the same shape. The egg of the guillemot is different, however. Its egg is pear-shaped, being blunt at one end and pointed at the other. Guillemots breed on sea cliffs and lay their eggs on steep ledges. The peculiar shape of the egg prevents it rolling off the edge. If it becomes dislodged it just rolls round in a circle.

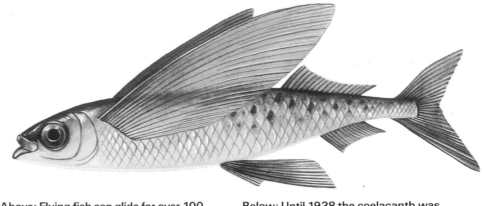

Above: Flying fish can glide for over 100 metres, using their specially developed fins. This ability helps them escape when being pursued by predators under the water.

Below: Until 1938 the coelacanth was thought to have been extinct for 60 million years. This 'living fossil' is now known to live in deep water in the Indian Ocean.

Coelacanth

Below: The goliath beetle of Africa is the heaviest insect on earth. Weighing over 100 grams it is heavier than many small mammals and birds.

Goliath beetle

Axolotl

Above: The axolotl is a remarkable amphibian related to salamanders. It lives its life as a permanent larva, and uses feathery gills with which to breathe. Even more remarkably, it can even breed while still a larva.

Below: Most species of bat are able to fly in complete darkness, easily avoiding obstacles and catching insects on the wing. They use echolocation to find their way around, although they are not in fact blind.

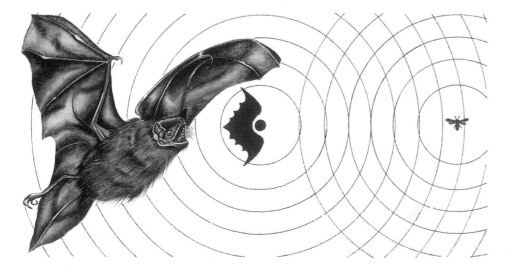

Cactus wren

Above: The cactus wren is a rare example of an animal which uses a tool. By holding a stick in its beak, it prises insects out of crevices in bark.

43

Living Together

We have already seen how the world of plants and the world of animals are closely interwoven together. Without plants, no animals could survive. Many animals would have no source of food or shelter, and this would mean no food for the other animals which prey upon them. Likewise, many plants rely on animals for their survival. Without insects and other animals, many flowers would not be pollinated nor would their seeds be dispersed. Insectivorous plants such as the sundew and the Venus fly trap must also catch and digest insects and other small creatures in order to obtain the nitrogen which is essential for their healthy growth.

Many animals also need the help of other animals to help them avoid predators or to help them find food. For this reason some species join together in great herds. Sometimes, however, animals which are quite unrelated join together to improve their chances of survival.

Below: Grazing animals, like these herds of buffalo on the American plains, join together in great herds for protection. The herd guards the youngest members which might fall victim to predators, and each animal is always on the lookout for any signs of danger.

Oxpeckers

Water dikkop

Spur-wing plover

PLANT AND ANIMAL PARTNERSHIPS

Although most of the partnerships in nature are between different species of animals, or between different species of plants, there are some partnerships in which a plant and an animal live together. Many aquatic animals, such as corals or the freshwater creatures known as Hydra, contain green algae within their bodies. The algae have a safe place in which to live, and in return they provide oxygen and absorb the various waste materials produced by the animals. Within the bodies of many animals live bacteria. These help to break down the cellulose found in plants and so enable the animals to digest grass.

Anemone

Hermit crab

Clown fishes

Anemone

Above: The hermit crab often carries an anemone around on its shell. The anemone protects the crab, and in return shares some of the crab's food.

Above: Clown fishes are brightly coloured inhabitants of coral reefs. They feel quite safe swimming among the deadly stinging tentacles of anemones which also inhabit the reef. The anemones let the clown fishes swim among their tentacles to escape predators, in return for ridding them of parasites.

Animal Partnerships

In the Animal Kingdom there are many examples of animals living together for the benefit of one, or both, partners. The simplest form of this behaviour is when one animal spends its life living close to another animal for its own benefit. Birds such as cattle egrets ride on the backs of grazing animals as they walk slowly through the long grass. As they walk, they disturb insects and other creatures which the egrets then swoop down to feed on. Although the grass-eating animals do not themselves benefit from the

Top left: Oxpeckers are African birds which are allowed to feed on the skin parasites of rhinoceroses. In return, the oxpeckers alert the rhinoceros of danger.

Left: Spur-wing plovers and dikkops help keep crocodiles free of parasites.

association, they do not suffer either.

Sharks are often attended by fishes known as remoras. The remoras attach themselves to the sharks by means of suckers on their heads. They eat the scraps left over by the shark when it feeds, which in return uses the remoras as a 'vacuum cleaner' service, for they remove parasites from the shark's skin.

Sometimes two different species of animals rely so much on each other for food or protection that they are unable to live so successfully on their own. This condition is know as symbiosis. There are many examples of symbiosis in the Animal Kingdom. The partnerships shown on this page between the hermit crab and the anemone, and between the clown fishes and the anemone are two.

Female mosquitoes transmit the disease called malaria. The mosquitoes feed on the blood of man, which they obtain by inserting their mouthparts into blood vessels near the skin. As they do so, they inject into the bloodstream tiny, single-celled parasites called trypanosomes. Trypanosomes enter the red blood cells of humans and multiply. After a time, they burst from the cells and into the bloodstream, producing the familiar malarial fever. Some of the trypanosomes pass to another mosquito when it bites a victim, ready to be passed on to another human.

Index

Illustrators
Mike Atkinson, Jim Dugdale, Ron Jobson, Linden Artists Ltd.,
John Marshall, Bernard Robinson, Frederick St. Ward,
Mike Saunders and David Wright.

Cover illustrations by
Graham Austin/Garden Studio

British Library Cataloguing in Publication Data

Dempsey, Michael W. (Michael William)
  The World of animals.
  I. Animals.
  I. Title II. Tony Truscott Designs
  591

  ISBN 0-7235-4319-4

Copyright © 1990 World International Publishing Limited.
All rights reserved. Published in Great Britain by
World International Publishing Limited,
an Egmont Company, Egmont House, PO Box 111,
Great Ducie Street, Manchester M60 3BL.

Printed in Singapore.

ISBN 0 7235 4319 4